PARROTS, MACAWS & COCKATOOS

*There's more to parrots
than the bright splendor of macaws,
the satin softness of cuddly cockatoos,
the clever chatter of Amazons and African greys*

*Explore the hidden life of parrots in the wild
how they travel and feed in flocks,
how they choose mates and care for their young,
how and why they communicate*

*Learn what you can do to ensure the survival
of these lovable, highly endangered birds*

TEXT
Vicki León
PHOTOGRAPHS
R. H. Armstrong, Stanley Breeden, Jane Burton, John Chellman,
Ralph Clevenger, E.R. Degginger, Michael Dick, Clayton Fogle,
Richard Hansen, R.F. Head, Kevin Horan, M.P. Kahl, Zig Leszczynski,
Tom Mangelsen, C. Allan Morgan, Dr. Charles Munn, Robert Pearcy,
Fritz Prenzel, George Schaller, Rod Williams, Art Wolfe, Belinda Wright

DESIGN
Ashala Nicols Lawler

SILVER BURDETT PRESS

© 1995 Silver Burdett Press
Published by Silver Burdett Press.
A Simon & Schuster Company
299 Jefferson Road,
Parsippany, NJ 07054
Printed in the United States of America
10 9 8 7 6 5 4 3 2 1

CLOSE-UP
A Focus on Nature

SILVER BURDETT PRESS
© 1995 Silver Burdett Press
Published by Silver Burdett Press.
A Simon & Schuster Company
299 Jefferson Road, Parsippany, NJ 07054
Printed in the United States of America
10 9 8 7 6 5 4 3 2 1

Library of Congress
Cataloging-in-Publication-Data
León, Vicki, 1956-
    Parrots, macaws & cockatoos / by Vicki León;
photographs by R.H. Armstrong...[et al.].
    p.cm.-- (Close up)
    ISBN 0-382-24898-8 (LSB)
    ISBN 0-382-24899-6 (SC)
    1. Parrots–Juvenile literature. 2. Macaws--
Juvenile literature. 3. Cockatoos--Juvenile litera-
ture. [1. Parrots. 2. Macaws. 3. Cockatoos.]
I. Armstrong, R.H.,ill. II. Title. III. Title: Parrots,
Macaws, and Cockatoos. IV. Series: Close up
(Parsippany, N.J.)
QL696.P7L46 1994
598.71--dc20
                                        94-30908
                                        CIP
                                        AC

Parrots, macaws and cockatoos seem as familiar to us as movie stars or TV celebrities. We tend to think of them as feathered performers: beautiful, extroverted, colorful, and talkative. And yet most of us know much less about the true nature of parrots than we do about our favorite actors or athletes.

To date, human celebrities show no signs of becoming endangered. Neither do parrots in cages. (Worldwide, more than 45 million budgerigars are kept as pets. Each year, an estimated 500,000 parrots of all kinds are imported into the U.S. alone for the pet trade.)

Wild parrots, on the other hand, are desperately threatened. Of the 325-plus parrot species in the world today, just a handful – notably the Indian ringnecked parakeet, the cockatiel, and the budgerigar – continue to thrive in the wild. All of the rest have been designated as either threatened or endangered by the Convention on International Trade in Endangered Species of Wild Fauna and Flora (CITES). Thirty-eight parrot species appear on CITES' "red list" of critically endangered species.

Over 20 million years ago, parrots appeared on this planet. Radiating out from Australia and the Amazon Basin, these tree-loving birds began to fill warm-climate habitats in both the Old and New Worlds. A few hardy species eventually made their homes in colder climates, from Tierra del Fuego at the wind-swept tip of South America to the snowy slopes of New Zealand. Today, Brazil boasts 70 parrot species; Australia, over 50. Other regions of high parrot concentration are New Guinea, the South Pacific, and parts of Africa, India, Central and South America.

Although they can be as imposing as a 40-inch-long macaw or as diminutive as a 4-inch pygmy parrot, parrots as a group share many similarities. They generally possess large hooked bills with hinged jaws, strong enough in bigger species to snap a broomstick. Parrots are zygodactylous, a handy word that means "possessing two toes facing forward and two facing backward." Useful for climbing trees, preening, and other matters, this arrangement also lets parrots grasp and turn objects with almost-human dexterity. Like humans, parrots

SULPHUR-CRESTED COCKATOOS (*Cacatua galerita*), PICTURED AT LEFT, LIVE IN AUSTRALIA. THEIR SUNNY, SOCIAL NATURES MAKE THESE BIRDS DESIRABLE AS PETS. THE SCALY-BREASTED LORIKEET (*Trichoglossus chlorolepidotus*), PICTURED ABOVE, ALSO HAILS FROM AUSTRALIA AND THE SOUTH PACIFIC. BRIGHT AND BRILLIANT, THIS MEMBER OF THE PARROT FAMILY FEEDS ON NECTAR AND FLOWER PARTS.

 THE BLUE-AND-YELLOW MACAW (*Ara ararauna*) RANGES FROM PANAMA TO ARGENTINA. THE SIZE OF A GOLF BALL WHEN BORN, THIS MACAW GROWS TO BE NEARLY THREE FEET LONG FROM ITS HANDSOME HEAD TO THE TIP OF ITS BLUE-AND-GREEN TAIL. CRACKING NUTS AND HARD SEEDS IS A CINCH FOR MACAWS. THE BEAK OF A HYACINTH MACAW, FOR INSTANCE, APPLIES UP TO 300 POUNDS OF BITING PRESSURE PER SQUARE INCH. PARROT BEAKS HAVE A SENSORY ORGAN AT THE TIP THAT MAKES PARROTS EVEN MORE ADEPT AT HUSKING THEIR FOOD.

tend to be left- or right-"handed." To pick up food and other objects, they favor one foot or the other.

During the thousands of years that parrots have been kept as pets by humans, they have been fed everything from sunflower seeds to dog chow to *chica*, an Indian beer made from sweet potatoes. Field studies now show that parrots are opportunistic omnivores, eating an astonishing range of seeds, fruit, bulbs, nuts, berries, worms, and insects. The kind and variety depend on parrot species and the season. Lories, for instance, concentrate on nectar and flower parts, using specialized brushy tongues to lap liquids. Parrots with huge strong bills, such as palm cockatoos and macaws, include hard-to-open nuts and seed pods in their diet. Small ground feeders like cockatiels and budgerigars pick at grass seeds.

The most important discovery made in recent years is that wild parrots spend most of their lives not just locating food but playing with it. Attracted by color, shape, size, and texture, parrots use foods as important outlets for their curiosity and sense of play. (You might say that parrots – like many humans – live to eat, not eat to live.) Parrots possess only 5% of the taste buds we do, and their sense of smell is thought to be poor. But their vision and tactile senses make up for it. Parrots see colors and distinguish shapes very well. You may have seen them cock their heads to peer at you; this focuses their fovea – an area packed with vision cells – on an object. The parrot also has a busy little tongue, as clever, plump, and inquisitive as a toddler's fingers. Parrot tongues and toddler fingers are used in much the same way for much the same purpose: exploration.

Intensely social birds, parrots often mate for life, a life which can be many decades long in the wild. (Researchers have little data on life spans in the wild but lots of statistics on the longevity of captive parrots, which sometimes outlive several generations of human keepers.) Most parrots feed, travel, roost, and socialize in noisy flocks, separating only to breed and nest. Although there are exceptions, parrots prefer to nest in tree cavities, logs, burrows, or other ready-made hollows. Except for lovebirds and monk parakeets, parrots don't bother making elaborate nests to cushion their white glossy eggs. They simply line the nesting quarters with wood chips, twigs,

A MALE GRAND ECLECTUS (*Lorius roratus*) IS NOT SHY ABOUT VOCALIZING, AND GIVES A RASPY SHRIEK. THESE SOUTH PACIFIC NATIVES HAVE A TYPICALLY PARROTLIKE BEAK, WHICH THEY USE ALMOST AS A THIRD FOOT TO CLIMB TO THEIR NESTS HIGH IN TREE HOLES. THEIR FEATHERS ARE UNUSUAL, ALMOST FURRY IN TEXTURE.

 RAINBOW LORIKEETS (*Trichoglossus haematodus*) LOVE TO BATHE. IN THE WILDS OF AUSTRALIA, THEY MOST OFTEN DO SO IN WATERHOLES AND IN RIVERS. HIGHLY SOCIAL BIRDS, THEY ADORN THEIR FAVORITE FEEDING TREES AND FLOWERING SHRUBS LIKE CHRISTMAS ORNAMENTS. RAINBOW LORIKEETS ARE LIKE MOST PARROTS IN THEIR NEED

or other simple items. Larger birds, such as macaws, do not breed every year, and their offspring are fewer. Smaller parrots, such as cockatiels, breed yearly or sometimes more often. Their clutches can produce three to eight young at a time.

Baby parrots make a shocking contrast to their glossy, showy parents. Like other altricial birds, parrots emerge looking half-finished. Blind, pink, and naked, they do little but squawk, eat, excrete, and grow. In a few weeks, their eyes open, feathers sprout, and it's hard to believe they ever resembled blobs of Silly Putty. By the time they are fledged, parrots look quite like adult birds. This is the age in which parrots, like other birds, establish dominance within their group. Even captive birds with no other parrots as companions try to establish a pecking order with their human keepers. (Some parrot experts liken it to the "terrible twos" developmental stage that human children go through.)

Unlike many bird species where showy males and drab females are the norm, parrots don't exhibit much sexual differentiation. In fact, it is darned hard to sex certain species, as owners hoping to breed birds often find.

TO KEEP FEATHERS CLEAN. TO BATHE, PARROTS USE WATERFALLS, TROPICAL SHOWERS, WET LEAVES, STREAMS – EVEN DUST. BATHS ARE FOLLOWED BY THOROUGH GROOMING OR PREENING.

A couple of female parrots are even more splendid than the males: the eclectus female, for instance, wears brilliant ruby red plumage, which contrasts nicely with the lime green of the male bird.

W e're used to seeing parrots in cages, where they stand out from their surroundings. But bright plumage actually serves as camouflage for many wild parrots. Quite often, their habitat is ablaze with vivid flowers and ripening fruit. Observers have often seen flocks of wild parrots fly into feeding trees, literally disappearing into the dense foliage and dappled shade. Parrot coloration – and their ability to see colors – also play a role in communication. For instance, parrots may threaten one another by puffing their feathers to appear bigger, which also shows more color. Sometimes an aggressive color like red is found on a prominent part of the parrot's body, like its shoulders. When the bird ruffles its feathers and leans forward, the message given is "Go away!"

Even the largest parrots have natural enemies. For adult birds, hawks and other raptors are the greatest threat. Young birds still in the nest get attacked by snakes, butcherbirds, and other predators. Drought, fires, hurricanes, and other natural disasters sometimes wipe out parrot flocks in Australia, the Caribbean, and other locales. As with other living creatures, the double-barreled effect of human interference on habitat and wild populations is by far the biggest threat to all parrot species.

Not all parrots are brilliantly colored. There are coal-black lories, olive-drab New Zealand parrots, grey African parrots, and a few others. They do seem to be the exceptions in this rainbow-colored family.

Although they do not migrate, most parrots are strong, fast flyers. At dawn, they fly in Technicolored flocks to search for food and eat all day, returning to the same roosting trees to spend the night. To keep their plumage airworthy and parasite-free, most species groom and bathe often. Parrots love to be in tropical rainstorms, spreading their wings and tail in a characteristic posture to catch the raindrops. Parrots also bathe high above the ground, where the leaves of rainforest canopies form little pools. On the dry plains of Australia, flocks of parakeets, corellas, and other species splash in noisy and glorious unison at waterholes. Some species even prefer to dust-bathe.

Beauty aside, it may be their ability to imitate human speech and other sounds that have made parrots such desirable pets throughout history. Opinions and individual birds differ, but it's clear that many species, especially the African grey parrot, the Indian ringnecked parakeet, the budgerigar, and the Amazon parrots, are excellent talkers. Much seems to depend on a given bird's personality and the humans to which it decides to relate. There are loquacious cockatoos and Senegal parrots. There are many more which are uninterested in talking.

It was once thought that parrots used their vocal talents in a very limited way in the wild. If that were so, it would make their abilities in captivity even more puzzling. Field research is beginning to fill the gaps. A 1970s study of Amazon parrots showed that they vocalize in local "dialects," much like the killer whale pods of British Columbia. These patterns are then learned by the young of that group. Parrots call often while in flight; these cries may help point out food to the flock.

Parrots have characteristic alarm cries. Cockatoos and other parrots are known to post "sentinel" birds, who watch while the rest of the flock is eating and squawk at danger.

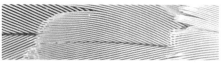

THE 6-INCH PEACH-FACED LOVEBIRD (*Agapornis roseicollis*) COMES FROM AFRICA. LOVEBIRDS ARE AMONG THE FEW PARROTS TO BUILD NESTS BY CARRYING BUILDING MATERIALS STUCK AMONG THEIR RUMP FEATHERS OR THEIR CHESTS. AS BEFITS THE NAME, MATED LOVEBIRDS SHOW STRONG INTEREST AND AFFECTION FOR EACH OTHER.

The field research of Dr. Charles Munn in South America has turned up an interesting benefit derived by the parrot playing sentinel. When it gives an alarm, large numbers of parrots fly off, in the process knocking insects loose from foliage. This gives the sentinel bird a "bonus" in the form of easy-to-forage bits of protein.

Unlike humans, parrot sounds are formed primarily in the syrinx, not the larynx. Parrots do not use their tongues or mouths for speech.

Long-term research on the mental abilities of parrots is proving even more eye-opening. The work of ethologist Dr. Irene Pepperberg in Illinois has shown that parrots don't just "parrot" human speech. In open-ended studies with Alex, an African grey parrot, she has demonstrated that non-primates – such as parrots – are capable of abstract thought.

"In every study that we've completed in the last eleven years," says Dr. Pepperberg, "Alex has been shown to have abilities comparable to other animals – such as dolphins and primates – that have been tested in the same kinds of cognitive studies."

What does that mean to us? Like other parrots, Alex has an extensive vocabulary, and often makes remarks where and when they are appropriate. Alex can correctly name over 40 objects, identify and class them by color,

material, and shape, and pinpoint the ways, if any, in which they are the same or different from one another. He can also recognize quantities of up to six objects. These findings give a scientific basis to something that many parrot owners already believe – that their pets do more than mimic. Parrots process information, form concepts, make decisions, and communicate – not on a human level, but certainly at a more complex level than was previously thought.

Because of their social nature in the wild, parrots show great capacities for emotional attachment – yet another reason why humans have found them irresistible. Parrots are "huddle species," a word that perfectly describes their penchant for closeness. In the wild, parrots large and small do almost everything together. Huge macaws fly in pairs, wingtips almost touching. Little hanging parrots roost side by side, upside down. Mutual grooming – called alloppreening – is one of their most important activities. Parrots often use body language to invite preening or reduce tension between birds. Lowering the head (one of the areas a parrot cannot preen on its own body) asks for grooming. A raised foot or crest can mean "Give me room!" Other behaviors help cement the pair bond. Lovebirds and other parrots often "courtship feed," offering their mate food brought up from their crop, just the way baby birds are fed. Caged parrots without mates or companions sometimes

make this perfectly normal love offering to human owners, their surrogate mates. As parrot fanciers know, certain birds stand out because of their capacity to receive and give affection. Lovebirds, for instance, can develop very close bonds with certain other lovebirds and humans. Cockatoos, macaws, Amazons, budgerigars, and other parrots are able to imprint on humans and form lifelong emotional attachments. Not only do they seem to enjoy physical closeness, these birds are adept at learning a repertoire of vocalizations, acrobatic stunts, and humorous bits of business to keep their humans nearby. No matter how loving these inter-species relationships may be, it's wise to remember that we humans are only stand-ins for a parrot's mate and its flock. Learning about the true nature of parrots and their way of life in the wild is critical to meeting their needs in captivity.

THE BLUEBONNET PARROT (*Psephotus haematogaster*) OF AUSTRALIA NESTS IN DEAD TREES, FEEDING HER YOUNG WITH FOOD FROM HER CROP. THE NEW WORLD ORANGE-FRONTED PARAKEET (*Aratinga canicularis*), AT LEFT, ALSO NESTS IN TREES BUT LIKES CACTUS AND TERMITE MOUNDS AS WELL.

he parrot family contains hundreds of interesting species, a surprisingly varied bunch considering how closely the entire group is related. The smallest members are the Australian budgerigar (often and incorrectly called "parakeet" in the U.S.), the pygmy parrots of the South Pacific, and the parrotlets, which range from Mexico to Paraguay. African lovebirds, conures from the New World, lories and lorikeets from Australia, and true parakeets fall into the medium-sized category. Parakeets include the Indian and Asian ringnecked family, and the Australian parakeets, such as the rosellas. Larger parrots include the Eclectus parrot, the family of New World Amazon parrots, and the African greys. Largest of all are the macaws. Their dove-sized cousins, the dwarf macaws, provide the exception. Cockatoos and their smaller, slighter kin, the corellas and the cockatiels, round out the parrot family. Fitting nowhere into the scheme of things and yet interesting for their habits and rarity are the bizarre parrots of New Zealand: the kea, the kaka, and the flightless kakapo.

Even smaller parrots tend to be well-fleshed birds that travel in flocks. These qualities, plus their tendency to stay near fallen companions, have made parrots attractive food items at different times and places. For millenia, Australian aborigines hunted and ate the budgerigar, a name which is said to mean "pretty good eating." The world's most popular caged bird, budgerigars, ironically, are nomadic. In vast flocks, they wander the dry interior of Australia, their movements dictated by availability of water and the grass seeds they prefer. Rainfall also influences their reproductive cycle. As soon as they reach an area of recent rainfall, budgies breed, often breeding a second time if rain falls again. Nesting in logs, burrows, or eucalyptus trees along riverbanks, budgerigars typically produce three to five eggs per clutch. If favorable weather permits, these 7-inch birds can hatch out, mature, mate, and produce broods of their own within six months. First introduced into Europe in 1840, budgies – then called shell, zebra, or undulated parrots – quickly became pet-lovers' favorites. Thanks to captive breeding efforts, today's domestic budgies are larger than their wild counterparts, more colorful, and probably longer-lived. It's not unusual for this dynamic little parrot to live fifteen years on a good diet. (Birds fed on

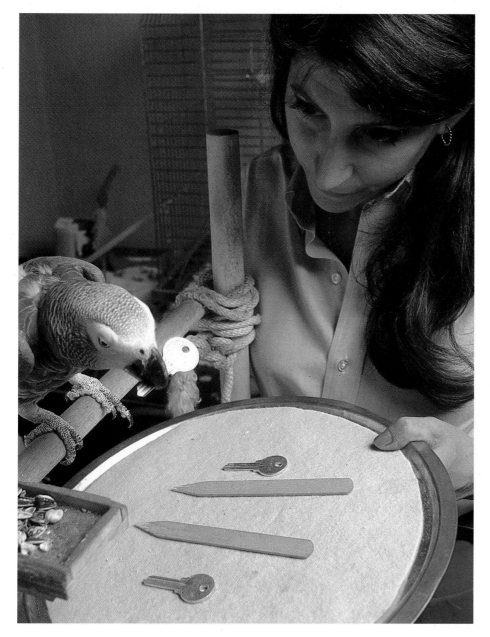

a seed-only diet have a three-year average life span.) Budgies come in lemon yellow, cobalt blue, cinnamon, and other hues, all of which derive from the bright green budgerigar of the wild.

The parrotlet, a charming bird about five inches long from its green head to its short wedgy tail, makes its home in wooded areas of Mexico and South America. Now being kept more as pets, captive-bred parrotlets would seem to be ideal companions. Small, pretty, and friendly, they have soft voices and some talking and mimicking abilities. In the wild, parrotlets feed in flocks, plucking fruit, berries, and seed with their beaks. Like budgies, they usually do not use their feet as "hands" for eating. Parrotlets nest in ground holes, hollow trees, and the occasional untenanted ovenbird nest.

THE KING PARROT OR PARAKEET (*Alisterus scapularis*) LIKES DENSE AUSTRALIAN WOODS; THE BRILLIANT SCARLET-HEADED MALE OUTSHINES THE OLIVE-DRAB FEMALE SOMEWHAT, BUT BOTH BIRDS ARE LIVELY AND FEARLESS. THEY REACH 16 INCHES. THE MUSK LORIKEET (*Glossopsitta concinna*), PICTURED BELOW, EATS EUCALYPTUS FLOWERS, NECTAR, SOFT FRUIT, AND THE ODD INSECT, LAPPING THEM UP WITH ITS BRUSH-TIPPED TONGUE.

14

into its rump feathers; Fischer's lovebird carries bark and leaves in its bill. Although mated pairs of lovebirds do shower most of their affection and attention on one another, the "love" is in short supply when it comes to other birds. Lovebirds can be aggressive to other birds and other species (including humans), especially during breeding season. At that time, you may see them fencing with their bills, squawking loudly, stretching, wing beating, or putting one foot onto the chest of another bird. Mated pairs, however, groom and feed one another in the most delicate fashion. The male also feeds the female while she is sitting on the nest.

Conures are versatile New World birds, occurring in colder parts of Patagonia and the Andes Mountains as well as in the humid lowlands of Brazil and Venezuela. They range in size from nine to 20 inches, but most fit neatly into the human hand. The Patagonian conure has an unusual nesting pattern for a parrot. It makes a den by digging a long tunnel with a chamber at the end of it into the side of a cliff or bank. Other conures, such as the Nanday, nest in populated areas on fenceposts, seemingly unbothered by human activities. A loud, social bird, the conure can live 20 to 35 years. Its varied diet includes fruit such as guavas.

In the running for most brilliant parrots? Lories and lorikeets. It isn't just their colors, which range from shocking pink to purple to acid green. Their feathers seem to have been finished with a high gloss, like the best Chinese lacquer. These dazzlers spend their days working over a variety of flowering plants, sipping nectar and nibbling pollen, soft fruit, blossoms, and any insects that fall their way. In the wild, flocks of lories and lorikeets frequent parts of Australia, Tasmania, Bali, and Indonesia. Besides their gaudy colors, lorikeets are interesting for their large repertoire of visual threat displays.

Due to their shyness, lack of success in captivity, and pocket size, pygmy parrots are largely unfamiliar to us. In their native South Pacific islands, pygmies crawl about tree trunks and hunt insects, often using termite nests as nesting areas.

The eight members of the *agapornis* family – commonly called lovebirds – live in Africa and Madagascar. These pleasingly plump parrots have bright green bodies and varied facial markings, depending on species. Some species prefer to live in small flocks at the top of trees; others, in the mountains. Still others are desert birds. They are unusual among parrots in needing a great deal of water to drink. One of the few architects among the parrots, lovebirds build two-room nests but are not choosy about site. The peach-faced lovebird carries building materials tucked

Not just aggressive at breeding times, lorikeets try to intimidate one another over food, nesting spots, and perches. A Cambridge study identified nearly 20 different threat gestures between opponents. Displays are ways of avoiding actual combat. The study showed that larger-billed, better-armed lorikeets have bigger vocabularies of threat gestures than smaller-billed ones. Because of their liquid diet and consequently messy droppings, lories have traditionally needed more care than other parrots. Newly developed powder diets have now made things easier, increasing the popularity of these clever birds as pets.

The ringnecked parakeets of India, Africa, and Southeast Asia have long fascinated humans. Slim, very clever at talking, and beautifully colored with distinct rings that mark the head from the body, these birds live in large flocks, feasting on ripe fruit and nesting in trees. The plum-headed parakeet is especially lovely; the male's head feathers resemble the bloom on a freshly picked piece of ripe fruit.

Many other medium-sized parakeet species are found in Australia. The scarlet king parrot (actually a parakeet) and the rosellas are standouts. Rosellas have neat markings and bright colors; several are predominantly scarlet. Living in habitats ranging from cold and snowy to hot and dry, all nine species eat seeds, have a musical call, and are excellent flyers. These parakeets are closely related to the smaller budgerigars and the grass parrots.

A New World parakeet of special interest is the monk or Quaker parakeet. Although it ranges from South to Central America, it has

also gained quite a foothold in Puerto Rico and parts of the United States. This has come about because escaped birds have managed to establish themselves. This bird is the only parrot to nest communally, building large, untidy, condominium-style nests of sticks. Prolific as well as hardy, the Quaker relishes a varied diet of blossoms, insects, fruits, seeds, and nuts.

A native of the Solomon Islands and other jungle regions of the South Pacific, the 14-inch eclectus parrot fooled humans into thinking that the red females and green males were totally different species until 1874. Besides its elegant coloration, the eclectus has most unusual feathers – more furlike than feathery.

Thanks to Christopher Columbus and a diet of childhood pirate films, Amazons are the birds we often think of when "parrot" comes to mind. Smart birds with chunky, predominantly green bodies, Amazons can be very friendly or much less so, depending on species. This varied family ranges over much of South and Central America. In Columbus' day, Amazons brightened the treetops of most Caribbean islands. Today, some Caribbean species are extinct, and others nearly so. Currently, 11 species of Amazons are listed as highly endangered. Others, such as the white-fronted Amazon, are still fairly common in their native lands. Yellow-naped and certain other Amazons learn to talk well. Well-cared-for birds have many years to do so, as they occasionally live to be 50 years old.

Like the hyacinth macaw and a few other species, some Amazons can be found in swampy areas. Amazons flock together for

food and socialization, separating into pairs to roost at night. This group of parrots shows the sexual maturation process in their feathers. Yellow-headed Amazons, for instance, get more yellow on their heads with each successive molt. It may take years for Amazons to reach full adult plumage. Their irises also turn from dark to bright orange as adults. Some birds are as small as 8 inches; the critically endangered Imperial Amazon can reach 20 inches or more.

More Wall Street than parrotlike in its sober gray plumage, the African grey wins human hearts by its amazing vocal abilities. Its speech is much clearer than most other parrots. And its ability and inclination to imitate the widest, weirdest variety of sounds is unsurpassed. There's a keen brain to go along with these talents, as we have seen in the long-term studies done with Alex. (He was chosen as a candidate for the study precisely because groundwork with other African greys had already been laid by several German ethologists.) African greys seem to possess many of the qualities (not always positive, either) that make parrots seem "human." They get bored; they can nurse grudges; and they can be very possessive. What are African greys like in the wild? Like other parrots, they live and forage in flocks, sleeping in tall trees. They nest in tree hollows, producing two to four eggs. The male is attentive, feeding the female while she is on the nest. Both parents work hard, bringing food to the young for up to four months.

THE WHITE-FRONTED OR SPECTACLED AMAZON (*Amazona albifrons*), A PLAYFUL PARROT FOUND FROM BELIZE SOUTH INTO SOUTH AMERICA, FORMS A FAITHFUL BOND WITH ITS MATE. THE TWO BIRDS PREEN EACH OTHER AND ENGAGE IN COURTSHIP FEEDING OFTEN. THE MALE ALSO EXHIBITS A BEHAVIOR CALLED EYE-BLAZING. IN RAPID-FIRE SUCCESSION, ITS IRISES CONTRACT AND EXPAND REPEATEDLY, RESPONDING TO EXCITEMENT OR PERHAPS DELIGHT. AMAZONS INDULGE IN MOCK FIGHTING AND OTHER SOCIAL PLAY. THEY ALSO DISPLAY AGONISTIC BEHAVIOR, DISPLAYS WHICH MIX FEAR AND THREAT. THE YELLOW-SHOULDERED AMAZON PARROT ON PAGE 40, FOR EXAMPLE, IS NOT JUST BEING CUTE; HE IS WARNING ANOTHER BIRD TO BACK OFF.

Deep in the jungle, as many as 15 different species of macaws and parrots gather daily at certain riverbanks called "culpas" by the South Americans. Their purpose? To eat riverbank clay, believed to contain a substance which counteracts toxins. Nibbling clay allows macaws and other parrots to include poisonous seeds, unripe fruit, and other unlikely things in their diets. The daily comings and goings of red-and-green macaws (Ara chloroptera), blue-and-yellow macaws (Ara ararauna), rare scarlet macaws (Ara macao), and a host of other noisy, gregarious, and showy parrots has to rank as one of the most spectacular sights in nature.

Early morning, somewhere in the heart of the Amazon. Above the forest canopy, you see flashes of color so bright they appear man-made. Turquoise. Day-Glo yellow. Blood-red. Red with shocking blue and acid green. Macaws. Besides color, the sight of their great beaks and their long tails, trailing like colored arrows, is unmistakable. So is their noise in flight; even at 35 mph, they yell like banshees. As they move from roosting trees to their feeding grounds, the macaws fly in tight formation, wings almost touching. Once they begin to feed, the great birds fall almost silent. Only a rain of plant debris, falling to the forest floor, reveals their presence.

Few of us are lucky enough to have seen macaws, the largest members of the parrot family, moving wild and free in their Central and South American habitats. But the pioneering studies of scientists such as Dr. Charles Munn and Dr. Robert Ridgeley have given us vital clues about their lives.

A fascinating aspect of macaw life is their diet. Field studies now show that macaws, along with other parrots, eat dozens of kinds of seeds, fruit pulp, and flowers. The scarlet macaw uses at least 38 kinds of plants. More interesting than the variety is the fact that many of the seeds and fruits are either toxic or so unripe they are loaded with tannins. With their steely beaks, macaws (and certain other parrots) are able to cut through, peel, and dissect nearly impregnable seed pods and fruits. So how do macaws and other parrots keep healthy on a diet loaded with toxins? They feed daily on riverbank clay, a diet supplement that scientists believe may absorb or detoxify the poisons.

As long as there have been parrots, macaws and other species have probably congregated on remote riverbanks deep in the jungle. Even today, only a handful of trappers, scientists, and photographers have ever seen these vivid daily assemblies. Arriving in the morning, the birds approach the clay lick cautiously, lighting in nearby bushes and trees. After much squawking and discussion, the first group of parrots flies to the clay and begins nibbling. (Because parrots are tree species, their slow waddling gait on the ground makes them vulnerable to eagles, wildcats, and other predators.) As a further precaution, the birds do not light on the ground until their group numbers 30 or more. Macaws prefer even

BABY SEVERE MACAWS (*Ara severa*) AT 9 TO 16 DAYS: EYES JUST OPENED, FEATHERS BEGINNING TO SPROUT, CROPS BULGING WITH FOOD. VIGOROUS EVEN WHEN YOUNG, LITTLE MACAWS BEG FOR FOOD BY FLINGING THEIR WINGS AND GIVING LOUD CRIES. THE PARENT RESPONDS BY GRASPING BABY'S BEAK AT AN ANGLE; THE YOUNG BIRD PUMPS AWAY, TAKING FOOD FROM THE PARENT'S CROP INTO ITS OWN. CONTRAST THESE NAKED BABIES WITH THE SPLENDID ADULT PLUMAGE OF THE RED-AND-GREEN MACAWS (*Ara chloroptera*), ALSO CALLED GREEN-WINGED MACAWS, AT NEAR LEFT.

bigger groups. Dr. Munn has seen as many as 15 species at the clay licks, waiting their turn. After the smaller birds eat for half an hour or so, the larger birds take their places. From time to time, parrots on sentry in the treetops give an alarm and a great confused mass of color explodes into the air. This spectacle of noisy beauty takes place daily at clay riverbanks throughout the macaws' range.

The 16 remaining species of macaws include a number of smaller birds, called dwarf macaws. Large or small, many of the macaws are severely endangered; several are thought to be extinct in the wild.

Regardless of size, all macaws are characterized by strong beaks, long pointed tails, loud voices, and a facial area called the cheek patch. On the scarlet macaw, the cheek patch is naked. On the military macaw, the blue-and-yellow, and the green-winged, the cheek patch is adorned with lines of single feathers in a stitchery-like pattern. In some species, each bird's pattern is as unique as a fingerprint. As sensitive as they are intelligent, macaws signal anger or unease by blushing. Their cheek patches get quite noticeably pink.

Some macaw species move and feed in flocks; others do not. But all macaws are devoted family birds, mating for life and looking after their young even after they are grown. The most disturbing discovery made

 MILITARY MACAWS (*Ara militaris*), ALSO KNOWN AS GREAT GREEN MACAWS, LIVE IN THE DRY FORESTS OF MEXICO, ARGENTINA, AND OTHER LATIN COUNTRIES. THESE DROLL, DIGNIFIED BIRDS TRAVEL AND FEED IN FLOCKS. MILITARY MACAWS, AS YOU SEE ABOVE, ARE AMONG THE PARROTS THAT BLUSH. WHEN THE BIRD IS ANGRY, EXCITED, OR UNEASY, ITS CHEEK PATCHES FLUSH WITH COLOR. OTHER PARROTS, INCLUDING THE PALM COCKATOO, SHARE THIS INTERESTING TRAIT.

A SCARLET MACAW (*Ara macao*) PREPARES FOR SLEEP BY TUCKING ITS HEAD INTO ITS BACK FEATHERS. UNUSUAL AMONG MACAWS BECAUSE THEIR CHEEK PATCHES ARE COMPLETELY NAKED, SCARLET MACAWS ARE FOUND IN DIMINISHING NUMBERS IN SOUTH AMERICA AND MAY ALREADY BE EXTINCT IN CENTRAL AMERICA. MATED AND LOYAL FOR LIFE, SCARLET MACAWS MOVE IN FLOCKS OF TWO DOZEN BIRDS OR MORE, EACH BIRD FLYING SO CLOSE TO ITS MATE THAT THEIR WINGS NEARLY TOUCH. REVERED FOR CENTURIES BY AMERICAN INDIANS, SCARLET MACAW REMAINS HAVE BEEN FOUND IN ARCHEOLOGICAL SITES AS FAR NORTH AS ARIZONA.

about macaws is their low reproductive capacity in the wild. There may be as few as 15 to 25 young born each year to a group of 100 adult breeding pairs. Macaws do not breed annually; even when they do, their success rate is not 100%. On the other hand, well-cared-for macaws reproduce quite successfully in captivity. So the justification for taking these magnificent creatures from the wild just isn't there. Far better to support the trend toward ecotourism by visiting one of the reserves where you can now view macaws in the wild. Barely in the nick of time, countries like Brazil, Peru, Colombia, Suriname, Venezuela, and Ecuador are learning that macaws and other wildlife can bring them more revenue alive than imprisoned or dead.

25

 SALMON-CRESTED OR MOLUCCAN COCKATOOS (*Cacatua moluccensis*) COME FROM THE ISLANDS OF INDONESIA. OFTEN LOOKED AT BY PLANTATION OWNERS AS A SCOURGE BECAUSE OF THEIR TASTE FOR COCONUTS AND OTHER FRUIT, THESE COCKATOOS ARE MUCH PRIZED AS NOISY BUT AFFECTIONATE PETS. WHEN SURPRISED OR ANNOYED, THEY RAISE THE FAT WHITE FEATHERS OF THEIR CRESTS, REVEALING THE BEAUTIFUL CORAL OR SALMON COLORS OF THEIR UNDER FEATHERS. DESPITE THEIR CAPACITY FOR AFFECTION, COCKATOOS AND OTHER PARROTS CAN BE DISCONCERTING AS PETS. EMPATHETIC RATHER THAN SYMPATHETIC, THEY ACCURATELY PICK UP YOUR MOOD. A FEARFUL OR ANGRY HUMAN WILL IMMEDIATELY SEE THE SAME EMOTIONS REFLECTED IN THE BIRD.

With the dreamy delicacy of an Indian classical dancer, a cockatoo preens its lush creamy feathers. A fine cloud of dust emerges, product of specialized parrot preening feathers called powder downs. Undulating its highly flexible neck against its body, the cockatoo from time to time holds one foot up in what looks like admiration. This graceful gesture probably says "keep away" to another bird. It is one of a wide repertoire of body movements – some graceful, some acrobatic, some wildly comic – of the cockatoo.

These highly affectionate, beautiful birds come from Australia and islands nearby. All 18 species, including the smaller corellas and cockatiels, have distinctive head crests which stand up like Indian war-bonnets whenever the birds are excited, curious, wanting to intimidate, or feeling romantic. Larger cockatoos have stocky bodies, big heads, and bright shoe-button eyes surrounded by glove-soft bluish-white skin. At birth, cockatoos look much like other parrot species – piping pink bags with endless appetites. Weak and anxious as a newborn, the cockatoo quickly gains weight and confidence. In 40 days, it can raise its crest, flap its wings, and eat with its foot. Pink at birth, a cockatoo's feet, tongue, and beak quickly turn to shiny black. On some species, the feet and beak of the adults eventually turn almost white from the action of the powder downs. Cockatoos often sit more like penguins than other parrots. This is especially noticeable in the young, who appear to lean on their wings for balance.

This hunkering position is an innate behavior, a begging response for food.

Noted for being noisy, cockatoos moan, cry, screech, whistle, and imitate a variety of sounds, including human speech. Although not considered to have as much talking ability as other parrots, some cockatoos – bare-eyed and slender-billed corellas in particular – can and do speak quite clearly. In the wild, corellas creak like rusty hinges. Cockatiels' voices can be soft or grating. When begging for food, they can make a steady burr like a dentist's drill.

In their homeland, cockatoos live in great flocks in a variety of forest habitats. Sometimes they turn from their diet of native seeds, grains, berries, and fruits to farmers' crops. For this reason, a number of species – from the galah to the cockatiel – have been regarded as pests and shot in great numbers. Several cockatoo species include insects and roots in their diets. Most, however, are poor walkers, preferring to forage for food in trees.

Like many of the long-lived parrots, cockatoos usually mate for life in the wild. Their courtship displays make maximum use of their flexibility and their beautiful feather crests. Besides strutting and showing off their feathers, males weave their heads from side to side in a hypnotic figure-8 motion. Some species display in groups, or hang upside-down while displaying their crests. Once the honeymoon is over, cockatoos become dedicated parents. Both male and female help to incubate the eggs, taking turns for 25 days on the nest, located in hollow tree trunks.

Much sought-after as caged birds, cockatiels differ from cockatoos in several important ways. First is size: chunky cockatoos range from 15 to 34 inches. Willowy cockatiels never get bigger than 12 inches. Their long narrow wings and tail look very unlike the rounded, sculpted shape of the cockatoo. Cockatiels feed on the ground, picking up acacia seeds and grasses. They are nomadic flock birds, much like budgerigars. Nesting in eucalyptus hollows, cockatiels lay clutches of almond-sized eggs. Despite human predation, cockatiels are prolific breeders and have maintained their wild populations. In captivity, they are one of the easiest parrots to breed. The aborigines gave these slender, pretty birds a variety of melodic names: wamba, wee-arra, woo-ra-ling, and bula-doota are a few.

LEADBEATER'S COCKATOO (*Cacatua leadbeateri*), ALSO KNOWN AS MAJOR MITCHELL'S COCKATOO, IS IN THE RUNNING FOR FANCIEST AVIAN HEADDRESS. IT LIVES IN FAMILY GROUPS IN DRY PARTS OF AUSTRALIA. AT RIGHT, THE UMBRELLA OR GREAT WHITE COCKATOO (*Cacatua alba*) IS A GENTLE, 15- TO 20-INCH BIRD THAT INHABITS THE MOLUCCAN ISLANDS. IN THESE TWO SPECIES, BOTH PARENTS INCUBATE THE EGGS FOR ABOUT A MONTH. THEIR YOUNG STAY IN THE NEST FOR UP TO THREE MONTHS.

Our fondness for and fascination with parrots extends back several thousand years. Archeological evidence about parrots comes to us from the ancient Egyptians, Chinese, Persians, and American Indians.

About 500 years before Christ, a Greek physician named Ctesias wrote about a bird of India which could mimic both the Indian language and the Greek tongue. When the armies of Alexander the Great arrived in India several hundred years later, they encountered parrots – probably one or more of the beautifully colored ringnecked parakeet species – and brought them back to Europe. Their exotic charm, intelligence, and color made them highly desirable to wealthy Greeks, and later, to Romans. Kept in cages of tortoiseshell and silver, these parrots were taught to talk by special slaves. Once trained, parrots were considered more valuable than the slaves who taught them. In Roman Empire days, the most popular phrase to teach a parrot was "Ave Caesar!" or "Hail the emperor!" Teaching methods were sadly ignorant, however. In 50 a.d., Pliny the Elder, writing about the beliefs of his time, says of parrots: "Its head is as hard as its beak; and when it is being taught to speak it is beaten on the head with an iron rod – otherwise it does not feel blows." By the late Roman Empire, parrots had lost their scarcity value. Instead of being kept as pets, they were served up as novelty items at Roman banquets – possibly a kinder fate than being hit with an iron rod to learn to talk!

In medieval times, parrots from India were again a prerogative of royalty and the clergy. Rulers in colder climates kept them in cages of glass. It wasn't until Christopher Columbus' voyages to the New World that other varieties of parrots became known in Europe. Upon seeing the bright parrots and macaws of the Caribbean islands where he made landfall, Columbus no doubt considered them one more "proof" that he had reached India.

New World natives had long kept parrots for food, for ornament, and possibly as sentinels. In 1509, Spanish troops landed on one of the Caribbean islands to subdue its people. They were thwarted by tame parrots in the treetops, whose alarm calls alerted the natives to flee.

 A COMMON SIGHT IN AUSTRALIA ARE CORELLAS (*Cacatua sanguinea*), A SMALLER SPECIES OF COCKATOO THAT FLOCKS AND FEEDS NEAR WATER. AS SATIN-SOFT AS OTHER

COCKATOOS, CORELLAS
MAKE A CREAKY-HINGE
NOISE IN THE WILD. IN
CAPTIVITY, THEY ARE
NOTED FOR BEING ABLE
TO MIMIC HUMAN VOICES
BETTER THAN OTHER
COCKATOO SPECIES.

Once Captain James Cook and other explorers opened up Australia and the South Pacific in the 1700s and the 1800s, a new group of interesting parrots found an eager audience in Europe. Although Australia is home to 52 species, including such large birds as the cockatoo, it was the tiny budgerigar—often called "parakeet" by Americans—that made the biggest impact. By the mid-1800s, a budgerigar craze had swept Europe. Countries like France were importing 100,000 breeding pairs a year. Now even ordinary folks could own a little parrot. Before the turn of the century, Australia placed an embargo on some of its parrots to ensure that the flood of birds leaving its shores would not extinguish the species.

It was this wide public interest in brightly feathered, affectionate, talking birds that began the international pet trade existing today. Although budgerigars and the small cockatiels continue to be number one and two birds of choice for millions of parrot fanciers the world over, it is now the larger parrots whose wild populations are feeling the pressure of human acquisitiveness. Unlike budgies and cockatiels, the larger, longer-lived parrots breed very slowly. They also have fewer offspring. Thus they cannot replace themselves in the wild as quickly or as successfully as the smaller parrot species.

What is the net result of our growing passion for pet parrots? Nearly half a million parrots imported legally each year into the U.S. An unknown quantity of parrots smuggled into the U.S. or "laundered" by forging illegal export documents. And a large and growing list of parrot species that have vanished or are in imminent danger of vanishing.

Some of them have succumbed to pressures other than the pet trade. The Carolina parakeet, for instance. This attractive emerald-and-yellow bird once flew in chattering flocks of 200-300 birds, roaming the countryside from Virginia south to Florida, and as far west and south as Colorado and Texas. One of two parrots native to the U.S., the dove-sized Carolina parakeet loved fruit, grain, and corn. Its diet made it a prime target for farmers and hunters, who found it easy to kill because the birds roosted together in the hollows of sycamore trees. Habitat destruction and trappers who killed the Carolina parakeet for its pretty feathers completed the damage. The last wild flock was seen in 1938 in a South Carolina swamp. The last

THE HYACINTH MACAW (*Anodorhynchus hyacinthinus*), RARE AND BEAUTIFUL AS A LUSTROUS GEM, IS A GENTLE GIANT AMONG PARROTS. LESS SOCIAL THAN OTHER MACAWS, THE HYACINTH LIVES IN THE SWAMPS AND JUNGLES OF SOUTH AMERICA, NESTING IN BURITI PALMS IN FAMILY GROUPS OF FIVE OR SO. LIKE THE TROPICAL RAINFOREST PICTURED ABOVE, THE HYACINTH IS FIGHTING A LOSING BATTLE TO MAINTAIN ITSELF IN THE WILD.

HARDY SUN CONURES (*Aratinga solstitialis*) OF SOUTH AMERICA ARE THE CLOSEST LIVING RELATIVES TO THE NOW-EXTINCT CAROLINA PARAKEET OF NORTH AMERICA. MOST CONURES HAVE WHITE EYERINGS, MAKING THEM RESEMBLE CERTAIN SMALL AMAZON PARROTS. CONURES HAVE MANAGED TO FILL MANY ECOLOGICAL NICHES THROUGHOUT SOUTH AMERICA, FROM CHILLY PATAGONIA TO TROPICAL RAINFORESTS. LESS SUCCESSFUL IS THE ODD AND LOVABLE KEA (*Nestor notabilis*), A LARGE PARROT WHICH CAN WITHSTAND THE COLD OF NEW ZEALAND MOUNTAINS BUT NOT HUMAN PRESSURES ON ITS POPULATION.

Carolina parakeet in captivity died at the Cincinnati Zoo in 1914.

Another major factor in the decline of parrot species is a phrase you often hear today: habitat loss. Most parrots are essentially birds of the forest, nesting in trees and feeding on the products of trees. Human development, especially in the Amazon rainforest, the Central American cloud forest, and the wooded areas around Southeast Asia, the Philippines, and Australia's coastline, has gobbled up millions of acres of prime parrot habitat.

What, if anything, can be done about all this? Will zoo birds and caged parrots someday be the only evidence we have left to remind us of populations that once splashed their joyous colors across five continents?

Fortunately, it is not too late. Pet lovers and parrot breeders, for instance, have very clear choices today that affect the future of all parrot species. Rather than buy a bird that has been captured in the wild, you can choose a captive bred parrot. There are several good reasons to do this. Not only will you help

likely to want to talk. These birds often cost much more than wild birds but they are worth it. A parrot – especially a macaw, cockatoo, or other large species – should be viewed as a lifetime commitment, not a whim. (Regardless of what you read, parrots are not "easy care" pets. They require owners who take the trouble to educate themselves on parrot nutrition and behavior.)

Another humane option is to buy a smaller bird rather than a larger one. Smaller parrots, as we have learned, reproduce much more rapidly than larger ones. They also breed better in captivity. So the pressure on these populations is not as great. Smaller species offer just as much color, lovability, and intelligence as the bigger birds, and in some cases, more.

Captive bred parrots are becoming easier to obtain through a growing network of reputable breeders in the U.S. and elsewhere. Thanks to the efforts of these dedicated private breeders and to larger non-profit organizations such as zoos, the genetic future of many threatened parrot species has been safeguarded.

Public education is another area where individuals can make a big difference. Take the Caribbean islands of St. Vincent and St. Lucia, for instance. Because the birds were commonly shot for food, the Amazon parrots native to these islands had reached

preserve the species, you will end up with a bird that is tamer, healthier, and much more apt to live a long time. Due to the stresses of capture, shipment, quarantine, and exposure to other birds, as many as 99 out of 100 wild parrots may die within a year of their purchase in a pet store.

Captive bred, hand-reared parrots make the best pets because they have imprinted on humans, not other parrots. Viewing humans as their "parents," these parrots show great affection, not fear. They are also much more

a critically low number. Through an education program devised by English researcher Paul Butler, the people of these two islands developed an awareness and a pride in their native parrots. Although still not out of danger, the parrot populations of both islands are increasing. The success of this program hinges on a very important factor, one which needs to be part of all efforts to preserve parrots and other endangered species. It was aimed primarily at children. It is the children of today who will determine whether the world they leave to their children will continue to contain rainforests, hyacinth macaws, gorillas, blue whales, and other fragile species and ecosystems.

Reintroduction of native species into the wild is another strategy being used with certain parrot populations. In the U.S., the thick-billed parrot, once found in the pine forests of Arizona and New Mexico, had last been seen on American soil in the late 1930s. An ongoing program of captive releases into the wild, sponsored by the U.S. Fish & Wildlife Service, is bringing this cheerful-looking green-and-red parrot to desert skies again. Ironically, many of the birds being released are parrots originally confiscated from border smugglers.

Another program run by the New Zealand Wildlife Service seeks to create a predator-free environment on one of the smaller islands for the kakapo, an oddity in a region full of avian oddities. Without natural enemies for so many millenia that it lost the ability to fly, this chunky nocturnal bird is the only parrot species where the males display for the females at a distance. Assembling in groups or leks, the males give off great booming noises to attract mates.

Besides supporting efforts to save parrot habitats and parrots themselves, you can do one other very important thing. Whether you travel the world or travel vicariously by shopping at an import store, don't buy items made from wild parrots and other animals covered by the Convention on International Trade in Endangered Species (CITES). No matter how beautiful the feathers are, the price you pay for them is far too high. Extinction is a price everyone pays; a price no one can afford.

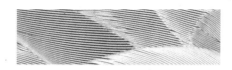

THICK-BILLED PARROTS (*Rhynchopsitta pachyrhyncha*), WHOSE EAR-SPLITTING CALLS ONCE RESOUNDED THROUGH THE PINE FORESTS OF MEXICO AND THE AMERICAN SOUTHWEST, ARE NOW BEING REINTRODUCED INTO ARIZONA BY THE U.S. FISH & WILDLIFE SERVICE. THESE CHUNKY, ATTRACTIVE PARROTS FEED ON PINE-CONE SEEDS AND NEST IN TREE CAVITIES OR ABANDONED WOODPECKER NESTS. WHILE EGGS ARE INCUBATING, THE MALE STAYS WITH THE FEMALE.

Photographers

R.H. Armstrong/Animals Animals: page 3
Stanley Breeden/DRK Photo: page 11, page 14
Jane Burton/Bruce Coleman Inc.: page 4
John Chellman/Animals Animals: page 27, page 40
Ralph A. Clevenger: page 17, page 31
E.R. Degginger/Animals Animals: page 9
Michael Dick/Animals Animals: page 5
Clayton Fogle: cover photo, page 12, page 23, page 24, page 26, page 36
Richard Hansen: page 22, page 29, page 39, inside back cover
R.F. Head/Animals Animals: page 16
Kevin Horan: page 13
M.P. Kahl/DRK Photo: page 1, pages 30-31
Zig Leszczynski/Animals Animals: page 32
Tom Mangelsen: pages 14-15
C. Allan Morgan: page 10
Dr. Charles Munn/VIREO: pages 20-21
Oxford Scientific Films/Animals Animals: pages 18-19
Robert Pearcy/Animals Animals: page 28
Fritz Prenzel/Animals Animals: page 2, pages 6-7, back cover
George Schaller/Bruce Coleman Inc.: page 35
Rod Williams/Bruce Coleman Inc.: page 25
Art Wolfe: page 34
Belinda Wright/DRK Photo: page 33

Special Thanks

My appreciation to the following people who so generously gave advice or acted as special resources for this book: **Jay Beckerman,** Director of the National Parrot Association; **Sally Blanchard,** avian consultant; **Dr. Irene Pepperberg,** ethologist, and **Robyn Bright,** her research assistant at Northwestern University; **Tani Smida,** California parrot breeder; **Tony Voyles**; **Pamela Higdon,** Managing Editor of *Bird Talk* magazine; **Rich Hansen**; **Clayton Fogle**; **Mary De Rosa,** Editorial Coordinator for *Animal Kingdom* magazine; **Wendy Worth,** Bird Department of the New York Bronx Zoo; **Chris Lazarus** of RareFinds.

— *Vicki León, author*

Helping Organizations & Recommended Reading

✦ **National Parrot Association**, 8 North Hoffman Lane, Hauppauge, New York 11788; phone (516) 366-3562. An international organization with a parrot hotline; publishes *Parrot World* magazine.

✦ **RARE Center for Tropical Bird Conservation**, 19th and the Parkway, Philadelphia, Pennsylvania 19103; phone (215) 299-1182. Non-profit group dedicated to the conservation of endangered New World birds and their habitats.

✦ **The Golden Triangle Parrot Club**, P.O. Box 1574, Station C, Kitchener, Ontario, Canada N2G 4P2.

✦ **Wildlife Conservation International/New York Zoological Society**, 185th Street and Southern Blvd., Bronx, New York 10460; phone (212) 220-5154. Publishes and sells color poster identifying endangered and non-endangered Amazon parrots.

✦ *Bird Talk* **magazine and** *Birds U.S.A.* **annual,** published at P.O. Box 6050, Mission Viejo, California 92690.

Where to see parrots in the wild

✦ **Costa Rica**: Guanacaste; Monteverde Reserve
✦ **Ecuador**: Napo River region
✦ **Peru**: the Manu Biosphere Reserve and the Tambopata Wildlife Reserve near Puerto Maldonado
✦ **Brazil**: jungle excursions from Belem and Manaus; Parrot Island, Oriole Island, Marajo Island; Planalto; the Rio Negro area
✦ **Suriname**: the nature preserves at Brownsberg, Raleigh Falls, Voltzberg, and Wia-Wia; Foengoe Island near Paramaribo
✦ **Colombia**: Leticia and Monkey Island, in the Amazon; Tairona National Park
✦ **Venezuela**: Canaima National Park, Orchid Island, Llanos
✦ **Australia**: national parks of Bunya Mountain, Hattah Lakes, Blue Mountains, Little Desert, Kakadu, Wyperfield, Lamington; the Currumbin Bird Sanctuary, Queensland; Ayers Rock and Alice Springs; and in park areas of Brisbane, Cairns, Darwin, Perth, and other cities
✦ **New Zealand**: South Island, Kapiti Island, Arthur's Pass National Park, Sinbad Valley

Parks & zoos:
a partial list

✦ **In the U.S.**: Albuquerque Zoo; Arizona-Sonora Desert Museum in Tucson; Audubon Park Zoo, New Orleans; Baltimore Zoo; Busch Gardens in Florida; Denver Zoo; Los Angeles Zoo; Milwaukee County Zoo, Wisconsin; New York Bronx Zoo; St. Louis Zoo; San Antonio Zoo; San Diego Zoo; San Diego Wild Animal Park; San Francisco Zoo; Santa Barbara Zoo; Sea World; Woodland Park Zoo, Seattle.
✦ **Outside the U.S.**: Singapore, Barcelona, Vancouver, B.C., Toronto, Jerusalem, Parque Loro on Gran Canaria.

AN INTIMATE LOOK AT THE FACE OF A HYBRID MACAW: THE PATTERNS ITS FEATHERS MAKE ON BARE SKIN LOOK LIKE AZTEC STITCHERY. SCIENTISTS ARE FINDING THAT THESE PATTERNS ARE UNIQUE TO EACH BIRD.

INSIDE BACK COVER:
THE CRIMSON-WINGED PARAKEET (Aprosmictus erythropterus), FOUND IN AUSTRALIA, NEW GUINEA, AND NEARBY ISLANDS, FLOCKS IN LARGE NUMBERS TO FLOWERING TREES.

PAGE 1: THE ROSEATE COCKATOO, ALSO CALLED GALAH (Eolopus roseicapillus) AN AUSTRALIAN BIRD, OFTEN EATS FOOD CROPS AND FOR THAT REASON IS CONSIDERED A PEST BY FARMERS.

Call or write for other books in our growing nature series:

Habitats:

Tidepools ❖ The Kelp Forest ❖ Icebergs & Glaciers
Tropical Rainforests ❖ Coral Reefs ❖ The Desert

Marine Life:

A Raft of Sea Otters ❖ Seals & Sea Lions
A Pod of Gray Whales ❖ A Pod of Killer Whales
Humpback Whales ❖ Sharks ❖ Dolphins

Bird Life:

Hawks, Owls & Other Birds of Prey
Parrots, Macaws & Cockatoos
A Dazzle of Hummingbirds

SILVER BURDETT PRESS

© 1995 Silver Burdett Press
Published by Silver Burdett Press.
A Simon & Schuster Company
299 Jefferson Road, Parsippany, NJ 07054
Printed in the United States of America
10 9 8 7 6 5 4 3 2 1